by Buck Peterson

Illustrated by

J. Angus "Sourdough" McLean

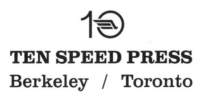

TEN SPEED PRESS
Berkeley / Toronto

DISCLAIMER: No state animals were injured in the production of this book. Injuries to state and many other animals are illegal and not encouraged. Injuries to cartoon animals are a different matter altogether. Any unauthorized use of this book is strictly forbidden.

Copyright © 2001 by Buck Peterson. All rights reserved. No part of this book may be reproduced in any form, except for brief review, without written permission of the publisher.

Illustrations by J. Angus "Sourdough" McLean
Cover and text design by Hicks + Son

Ten Speed Press
PO Box 7123
Berkeley, California 94707
www.tenspeed.com

Distributed in Australia by Simon and Schuster Australia, in Canada by Ten Speed Press Canada, in New Zealand by Southern Publishers Group, in South Africa by Real Books, in Southeast Asia by Berkeley Books, and in the United Kingdom and Europe by Airlift Book Company.

ISBN 1-58008-279-3
Printed in China
First printing, 2001

1 2 3 4 5 6 7 8 9 10 — 05 04 03 02 01

NATIONAL SUBURBAN SPRAWL INSTITUTE

A message from the executive director of the National Suburban Sprawl Institute

Dear Fellow Commuters,

As a nation, we are on the move—in our work, our play, and the place we call home. Many homeowners are following their dreams of leaving the city for greener pastures. One of the most important benefits of moving to the country is the opportunity to enjoy nature with our families. Members of the National Suburban Sprawl Institute, an advocacy organization of land stewards, have built many fine new roads that wind through areas where animals live. We are proud to play a widely expanding role in promoting the enjoyment of nature's blessings from within the safety of your automobile. Land reclamation in the US has dramatically accelerated in the last decade: more than three million acres of forest, wetlands, and other useless open space have been converted every year to more prosperous suburban use. We take our land stewardship very seriously and will move mountains to insure responsible mortgage holders a safe, orderly country lifestyle experience. We hope this colorful activity book brings joy to your everyday and vacation travels.

Introduction

Ladies and gentlemen, start your engines! From coast to coast and border to border, ROADKILL USA will help you and yours become road scholars of the natural world from the upholstered confines of your automobile.

The United States is a fabulous vacation spot, crowded with many wonderful animals. Our fast growing cities and states present unique opportunities for you to bump into your favorites. Many official state animals are featured in the following pages; however, some states are not included. North Dakota's winters are too cold and windy for any self-respecting animal. South Dakota's state animal, the coyote, is too busy ringing the neck of the state bird, the pheasant, to appear on these pages. Iowa has a state rock. Minnesota's state bird, the common loon (from a Scandinavian word meaning "unusual state politics"), and Delaware's blue hen chickened out to a Rhode Island Red. Nudging Hawaii's state bird, the néné goose is a big no no, but vacationers can make their own myna bird mixed grill on Oahu's north Highway 83. Idaho, Massachusetts, and New Jersey have a horse as state animal but you'd have to be a cousin of Missouri's state animal, the mule, to seek such an encounter. Never mind. You'll see a large enough gathering from the ark along our nation's high and bye-bye ways to play with.

Pack ROADKILL USA in your bags for a vacation at the beach, in the mountains, on the Great Plains, or in the national parks. Fire up your RV, ORV, or SUV for a bang-up vacation on the lumpy red carpet of suburban sprawl.

The illustrations in this book have been drawn (and some quartered) for your family fun. A useful guide to help you decide which colors to use: If you are traveling through these pages at night, color the roads, grass, trees, and your attitude toward getting to your destination in time to eat a solid black. For super realism, leave a few white holes, like eyes, about deer head high. If traveling by day, color the roads gray, the center lines bright yellow, the grass and trees a rich bright green (except when counter-indicated). Many of the animals (other than marine mammals and birds) should be colored brown/gray, darkest on top. Or bright red, depending on the circumstances.

Put the pictures in order by numbering them one to six.

Correct answers on page 62.

The moose is the state animal in the upper left and upper right corners of the USA. The long legs that work so well in deep snow put the moose in the driver's seat. Color the backseat driver red.

MATCH THE HEAD TO THE TAIL

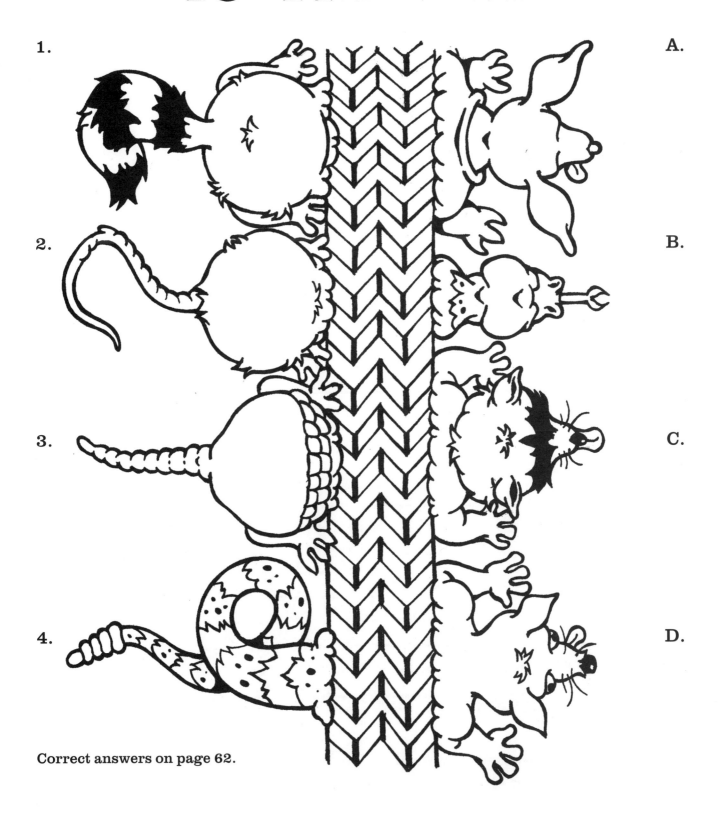

Correct answers on page 62.

Help Junior motor to the top of a mountain to butt heads with the Colorado state animal, the bighorn sheep. If Junior reaches the top, color him victor's red. Color the bighorn's head black and blue.

Survivors move on to gamble with Nevada's state animal, the desert bighorn sheep.

The grizzly bear is the state animal of California and is now found only in Hollywood. Grizzly fact: If you ram a 1,000-pound bear on the backlot, you'll see lots more stars than you expected. Color the tour cart's occupants red.

The whitetail deer is one of the most popular state animals, and the most likely large animal you'll run into on vacation. Identify and color the states that call this deer its own a bright, perky red.

1. South Carolina _____
2. New Hampshire _____
3. Mississippi _____
4. Ohio _____
5. Wisconsin _____
6. Arkansas _____
7. Michigan _____
8. Nebraska _____
9. Pennsylvania _____
10. Illinois _____

Correct answers on page 62.

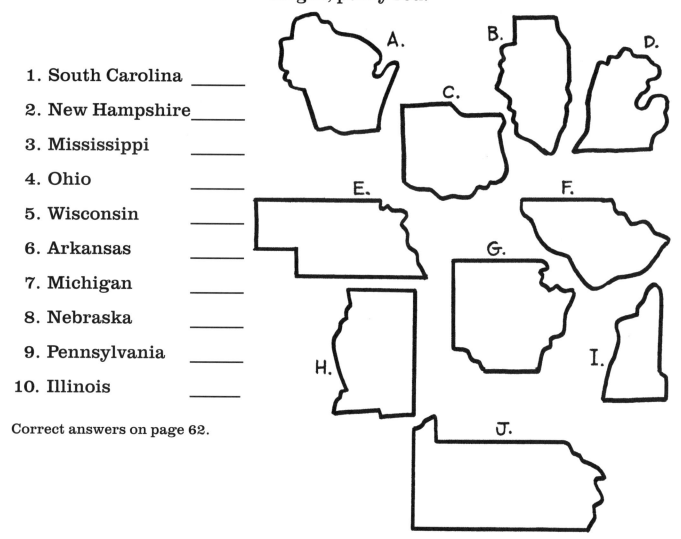

CONNECT THE DOTS

To see what kind of critter is caught in Billy's spokes, connect the dots from 1 to 15.

Start here.

To finish the picture, connect the dots from 16 to 46.

THE HIGHWAY PATROL

Guess the bird-brained scavengers.

Correct answers on page 62.

Whitetail deer live safely in suburban Connecticut, providing a steady supply of speed bumps for the golf set and visitors. Color the greens red.

What's the difference between the top and bottom pictures?

Correct answers on page 62.

MAD SCRAMBLE

Unscramble these letters to spell the most likely names of these animals, several with slightly scrambled features.

1. chunkmip   _____

2. gunrod qrueirls   _____

3. gorf   _____

4. hasenpfeffer   _____

5. catlope   _____

Correct answers on page 62.

WHADYA KNOW ABOUT POSSUMS?
TRUE OR FALSE

1. Possums are born dead on the side of the road. _____
2. Possum stew is noted for its wholesome flavor. _____
3. Opossums and possums are a lot alike. _____
4. Possum tails make real nice jacket ornamentation. _____
5. 'Taters and possum go real good together. _____
6. The mother's fur pouch makes a real nice purse. _____
7. The possum is our only native marzipan. _____
8. "We have met the enemy and he is us" is Pogo shtick. _____
9. People who 'et possum will 'et squirrel, too. _____
10. Old people like to play possum. _____

Correct answers on page 62. The player with the most correct answers colors the footprints red.

Of the three American vultures, a traveler is most likely to see the turkey vulture soaring, searching, and smelling for the "spoils" of your vacation. With dull bills and claws, nature's large avian street cleaners prefer soft, rotting animals. Color the vulture's bald head and talons red.

I SPY

Be the first one to spy a road critter and say "I spy with my little eye something red." Others in the car take turns trying to guess which animal you spotted. The first person to guess correctly gets to color the animal red.

Before the start of daylight savings time, animals could sleep safely in the early morning light. Color this possum's lights out.

Match the animal with the proper name of its group.
For example, a group of geese is called a gaggle.

1. Buffalo   A. Colony
2. Badger   B. Herd
3. Bear   C. Skulk
4. Crow   D. Knot
5. Deer   E. Cete
6. Fox   F. Murder
7. Hare   G. Sloth
8. Partridge   H. Down
9. Squirrel   I. Gang
10. Toad   J. Covey

Correct answers on page 62. The player with the most correct answers colors the flattened family member red. All other family members should be colored brown.

DISTRICT OF COLUMBIA

In these modern times, it is the beaver that chops down cherry trees inside the beltline of our nation's capitol, not to mention what they do below the beltline of presidential politics. Color this beaver's face red.

WHAT'S WRONG WITH THIS PICTURE?

Find the 12 things that are wrong with this picture.

Correct answers on page 62.

GUESS WHOSE FEET MAKE THESE TRACKS

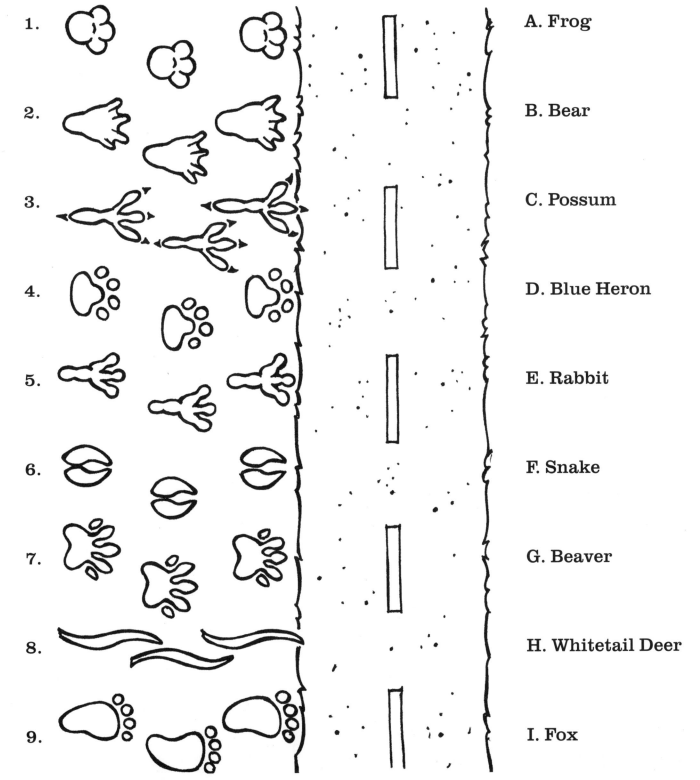

1.
2.
3.
4.
5.
6.
7.
8.
9.

A. Frog
B. Bear
C. Possum
D. Blue Heron
E. Rabbit
F. Snake
G. Beaver
H. Whitetail Deer
I. Fox

Correct answers on page 62.

Some coastal states have designated marine mammals as their state animal. For most vacationers, the only way to safely ram these whales is on a tour boat. Color the water red and the boat occupants black and blue.

"Rub-a-dub-dub, the grub's under the tub."

Turn to page 63 for a bonus match game.

WHO AM I?

This stinky pest deserves the full color treatment. Pick your palette and color him up to find out who's making that awful smell.

WHADYA KNOW ABOUT DEER?
TRUE OR FALSE

I know deer inside and out!

1. Mule deer are half mule and half deer.
2. Whitetail deer make good house pets.
3. Fawn meat can be cut with a fork.
4. Antlers make a deer horny.
5. Mule deer are half deer and half mule.
6. A buck in Canada is worth about 80 cents.
7. Mule deer are real stubborn but make good pack animals.
8. It's okay to go stag to the dance.
9. Bambi never lived.
10. Deerskin slippers are real comfortable.

Correct answers on page 63.
The player with the most correct answers colors the footprints red.

In the summer, animal young think it's safe to play their favorite games with friends in the neighborhood. Color them dead wrong.

Guess what an animal's average life expectancy was before roads.

1. Armadillo   A. 12 years
2. Whitetail Deer   B. 15 years
3. Frog   C. 16 years
4. Gopher   D. 3 years
5. Moose   E. 20 years
6. Field Mouse   F. Under 5 years
7. Possum   G. 2 years
8. Rabbit   H. Under 2 years
9. Raccoon   I. 10 years
10. Skunk   J. Same as raccoon
11. Garter Snake   K. 8 years
12. Squirrel   L. 12 years
13. Snapping Turtle M. 50 years

Correct answers on page 63.

ALTERED STATES

Draw a line from the animals on the left that match those on the right.

Correct answers on page 63.

The state animal of Maryland is a big dog, but not a big red dog. It's a big brown dog with extraordinary stamina and devotion. Guess what kind of dog it is. Color it brown and color the little yap-yap's face red with envy.

The state bird of Maryland is the Baltimore oriole. Color this flat feathered critter bright red.

WHADYA KNOW ABOUT RABBITS?
TRUE OR FALSE

1. Rabbit tails are 100% organic cotton. ____
2. The Easter Bunny was hatched by marketing. ____
3. A rabbit foot will bring its owner good luck. ____
4. What you hear about female rabbits is true. ____
5. The ears on a chocolate bunny are best. ____
6. Female rabbits like to wear eye shadow. ____
7. A jackalope is half rabbit, half cantaloupe. ____
8. The rabbit season opener is a bad hare day. ____
9. A March hare is mad in April, too. ____
10. Not all rabbits carry rabies. ____

Correct answers on page 63. The player with the most correct answers colors the footprints red.

During your trip, color the states where you see roadkill in red. Color the rest of the states and critters in your favorite colors.

THE UNITED STATES OF AMERICA

GOT A MATCH?

Circle the two animals most alike.

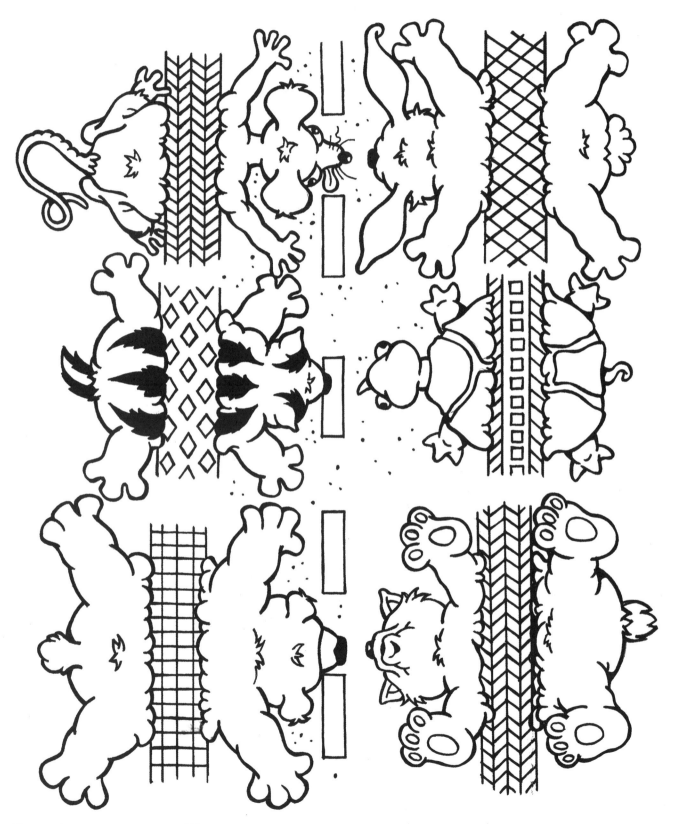

Correct answer on page 63.

In Montana, deer and antelope play peek-a-boom along the interstate ditches from dusk to dawn. Color the highways red.

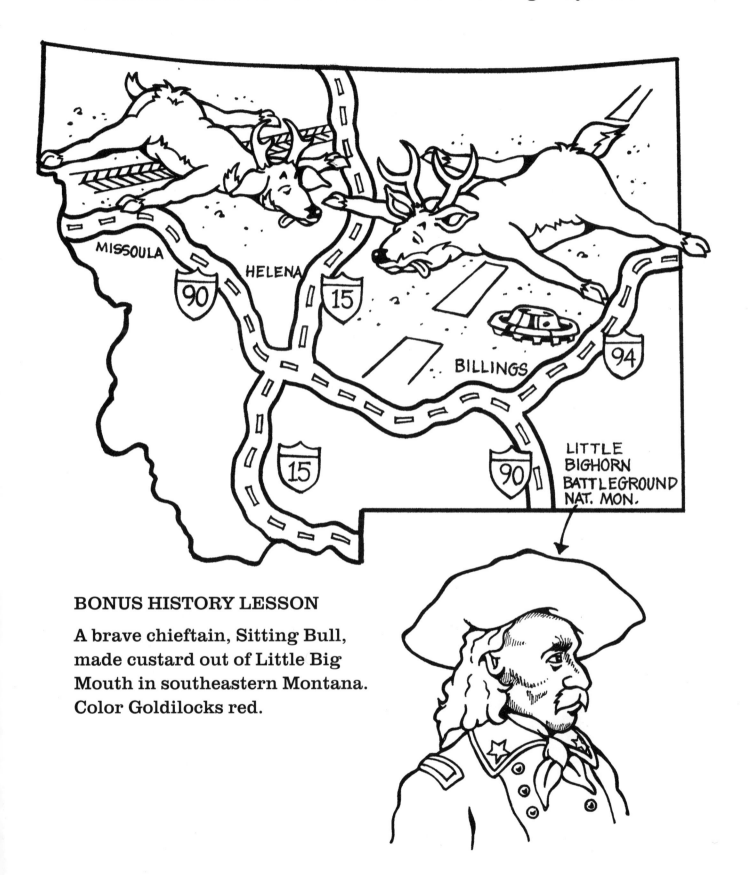

BONUS HISTORY LESSON

A brave chieftain, Sitting Bull, made custard out of Little Big Mouth in southeastern Montana. Color Goldilocks red.

AS THE WHEEL TURNS

Color the ancient animals in the petroglyphs found in Arizona's Petrified Forest National Park bright red.

North Carolina's state animal is the squirrel. Members of the squirrel family are commonly dismembered on the road.
The ground squirrel is often called a gopher. Color these great globs of greasy grimy gopher guts green.

"I like my squirrels ground extra fine"

RACE TO THE FINISH

A gamey game for two roadkill shoppers.

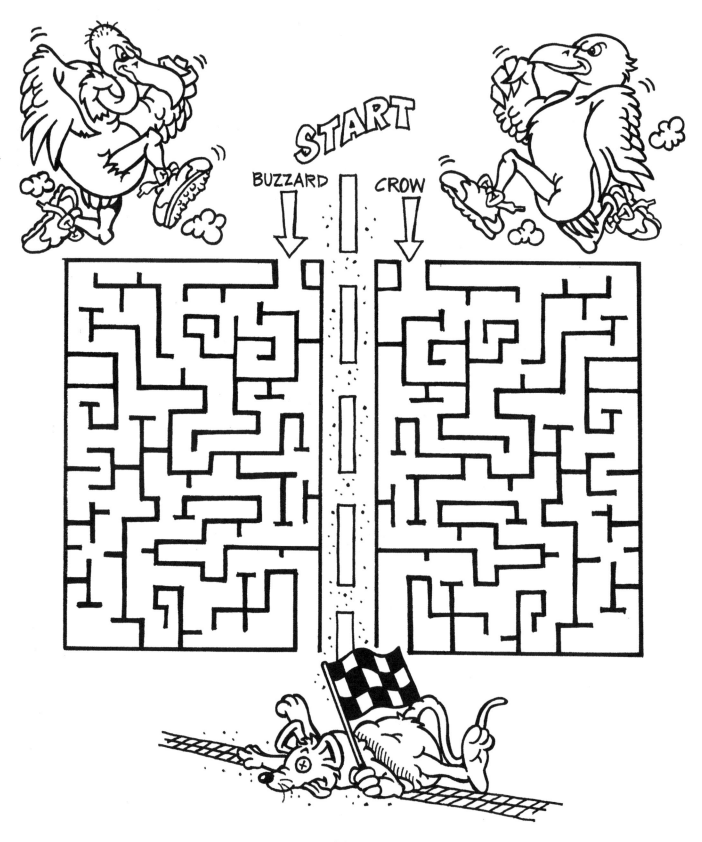

What's the difference between the top and bottom pictures?

Correct answers on page 63.

Help the Oregon state beaver find his way from Mt. Hood to his home at Crater Lake.

In the fall, trees in the northern states turn bright colors and many animals' thoughts turn to carefree romance. Color the leaves and the animal's tongue bright, bright red.

Fall foliage tours of the northeast are very popular. Color the carnage in rural Massachusetts, New York, and Maine, and Vermont's Green Mountains and New Hampshire's White Mountains a bright red.

WHADYA KNOW ABOUT DEER?
TRUE OR FALSE

11. If Bambi were real, he'd either be 78 years old or dead. ____
12. Fawn meat needs only a slight searing to seal in flavor. ____
13. Deer caught in headlights are playing blind man's bluff. ____
14. Long ago, a buck's skin was worth $1. ____
15. A stag party is lots more fun than church. ____
16. In the country, deer is called venison. ____
17. Deer have the emotions of building material. ____
18. Dear John letters are often very hurtful. ____
19. A new John Deere costs a lot of dough. ____
20. Not all deer in Connecticut spread Lyme disease. ____

Correct answers on page 63.
The player with the most correct answers colors the footprints red.

The black bear is the state animal of Louisiana, New Mexico, and West Virginia. However, motorists are more likely to have a "run-in" with a black bear in a national or nature park. If so, color your vehicle broken. Color the bear's stuffing red.

CROSSWORD PUZZLE

KEY: **Think RED!**

Across
1. Valor award
4. Hot dog grease
6. Emergency service
8. Government accounting fluid
9. Late travel
10. Valet apparel
12. Squirrel tree
13. Caught

Down
2. Biting insect
3. Search for fall month
5. Steinbeck's buzzard pickings
6. VIP treatment
7. Early comedian
11. Suburban deer food

Correct answers on page 63.

FIND THE BODY PARTS IN THE GUT PILE

RHODE ISLAND

The state bird is the Rhode Island red. When this big chicken crosses the rhode in the wrong place, color here a chick, there a chick, everywhere a chick, chick bright red. While you are at it, color the leaves on the red maple, the state tree.

DOUBLE JEOPARDY

For animals that dine roadside, objects in rear view are closer and larger than they appear. Color the entire page various shades of red.

GUESS WHO?

Connect the dots on this familiar holiday road pizza. No need to hurry. He isn't going anywhere.

The common raccoon is the state wild animal of Tennessee and a familiar pest everywhere else. The best time to nail the old coonskin to the wall is at night as it raids garbage cans and pet dishes. Color spaces number 1 black, number 2 red, and number 3 white.

Match mom to the common name of her offed-spring.
For example: Fox—Kit.

1. Skunk
2. Turtle
3. Raccoon
4. Frog
5. Hare
6. Goose
7. Moose
8. Snake
9. Porcupine
10. Rat

A. Gosling
B. Young
C. Hatchling
D. Kit
E. Mooseling
F. Neonate
G. Polliwog
H. Pup
I. Leveret
J. Kitten

Correct answers on page 63.

MEMORY GAMES

Study the page for one minute, then close your eyes and list all the items you remember. The one who can recall the most items wins. The one who can't remember anything should be punched in the arm real hard.

Red Letter Day

The first player calls out the name of the first roadkill seen that day. The next player has to name an animal that starts with the last letter of the first animal's name. For example, if the first roadkill was a deer, the next animal named would begin with the letter R, such as raccoon. The first player that cannot continue gets slugged in the arm and slugged real hard in both arms if another player can give the correct answer.

Who's Next?

This one is perfect for long road trips. The first player tries to guess which animal will get hit next. If that person is right, one point is given. If that person is wrong, one point is taken away. The person with the most points at the end of the day gets to sit wherever they like the next day in the car.

20 Questions

One player thinks of an animal that is commonly found along the roadside and doesn't tell the other players what it is. Everyone tries to guess which animal the first player is thinking of by asking questions with yes or no answers. If the animal is not guessed after twenty questions, the player gets to super size their next meal.

Memories are Made Out of This

The first player calls out the name of the first roadkill seen that day. They start a story with the roadkill adding one additional phrase. For example: "I was on the road to Houston and we ran over an armadillo which made a funny crunching sound." The next person repeats the first phrase, adding one additional phrase. For example: "even as we backed over it again." The game ends when no one can remember the point of the entire story.

99 Whitetail Deer on the Road
(sung to the tune of the familiar beer song)

99 whitetail deer on the road,
99 whitetail deer.
Step on the gas, don't let them pass,
95 whitetail deer on the road.
95 whitetail deer on the road,
Etc.
Continue the refrain until there are no whitetail deer left on the road.

Gory Story Time

Create your own story by filling in the blanks: Our family went on a vacation and I had to sit in the back seat with my _____ (descriptive term, sibling). My dad drives real fast and never stops when we want to. Coming around the bend in the road, we ran into a/an _____ (animal) that crossed in front of us. It made a noise like "_____!" My _____ (new descriptive term, sibling) cried out, "_____!" and Mom screamed, "_____!" Dad slammed on the brakes and _____ (name of pet) went flying over the front seat, knocking Dad's _____ (adult beverage) out of his hand. Dad said, "_____!" (naughty word) twice. It got real quiet in the car. We drove away fast so we wouldn't get in trouble with the police.

Car'toons

For every animal you run over, take turns naming a cartoon name for that particular animal. For example, if you hit a fawn, shout out "Bambi!" At the end of the day, the player with the most correct names gets the channel changer for the evening.

The Twelve Days of Vacation
(sung to the tune of the seasonal favorite)

On the first day of vacation, my daddy hit for me
A possum as far as you can see.
On the second day of vacation, my daddy hit for me
Two fat skunks and a possum as far as you can see.

Fill in the third through twelfth days as you motor along.

HEADS UP/TAILS LOSE

One player plays the animal, another the motorist. The object of the game is to see if the deer can safely walk from its quiet suburban sleeping quarters to the dining room and return. Flip a coin to start. To be realistic, the motorist can travel in both directions. Heads equals three or less spaces. Tails equals two or less. The deer can only turn around or backtrack after it has met its goal. Color any intersection red.

OH-OH!

The state small animal of Texas is the armadillo. Found throughout most of the southwest, the armadillo has the unfortunate habit of jumping up when it should lay flat. This gives Mother Nature's clean-up crew meals on the half-shell. Color either red or green for this state dish.

The "Don't Tread On Me" flag was used by the original 13 colonies during the American Revolution. Snakes are commonly found sunning on the open road. Guess the names of these tread-upon snakes and color them patriotic red.

1._____ 2._____

3._____ 4._____

Correct answers on page 63.

A fawn is lost in the suburbs. Can you help it find its way safely home without crossing a road?

Bumping into a buffalo, the state animal of Wyoming, in Yellowstone National Park will create a major headache—Yours! Color your vacation over.

WHADYA KNOW ABOUT WOLVES?
TRUE OR FALSE

1. The wolf is the Devil himself.
2. Little Red Riding Hood is still in critical condition. ____
3. A good wolf whistle gets the babes. ____
4. Wolves prefer beef raised in Montana. ____
5. It's not good to wolf down your food. ____
6. Wolves howl because their jaws are sore from ripping flesh. ____
7. Radio tracking collars cause canine cancer. ____
8. Domesticated wolves make good babysitters. ____
9. A she-wolf is the she-Devil herself. ____
10. Wolves like anything in sheep's clothing. ____

Correct answers on page 63. The player with the most correct answers colors the footprints red.

Answer Pages

The general answer to the general question of "What's black, white, and red all over?" is, the road-weary animal kingdom.

Page 5.   Clockwise from left: 6, 3, 4, 1, 5, 2.

Page 7.   1–C, 2–D, 3–A, 4–B.

Page 10.   1–F, 2–I, 3–H, 4–C, 5–A, 6–G, 7–D, 8–E, 9–J, 10–B.

Page 11.   In the sprocket's red glare, the bird is bursting in air.

Page 12.   A–Crow, B–Turkey vulture, C–Raven, D–Jay, E–Post Office symbol. The avian highway patrol is part of nature's larger clean-up crew that includes the mammal carnivores and the entire insect world.

Page 14.   The top picture was taken before Mom raced the kids to the soccer game. Note the SUV tracks.

Page 15.   1. Chipmunk—The lighter colored cheeks are a dead giveaway. In the audio version of this book, you'll hear them singing really cheesy songs. 2. After a while on the road, some of these animals are really hard to recognize. Our best guess is the Cascade golden mantled ground squirrel with a slight tail bob. 3. Frog. 4. Rabbit in a highly seasoned stew. 5. Polecat (skunk).

Page 16.   Number 1 should be true but isn't. Just goes to show you how much in life is often an illusion. All the other answers are true except for number 7. There is no such thing as a native marzipan. Even a marsupial knows that.

Page 20.   1–I, 2–E, 3–G, 4–F, 5–B, 6–C, 7–H, 8–J, 9–A, 10–D. In scientific terminology, a flattened group of a certain species is called a "mess" of animals. A regional variation of this term is a "heapin' mess" of animals.

Page 22.   1. The Chesapeake Retriever head belongs on page 30, not on Mt. Rushmore. 2. and 3. Who are those other two jokers? That guy's hairdo on the left is straight out of the fifties. 4. No Park Service tollbooth to see Mt. Rushmore. 5. The golfing bear is hitting a hole in one, which is impossible without an opposable thumb. 6. The turkey vulture is wearing sunglasses when no sun is out and 7. the glasses don't connect to its ears. 8. The palm tree has no coconuts. 9. The large trained bear by the side of the road belongs in a circus. 10. The animal with a hat in the middle of the road is not dead—no tire tracks. 11. Where's the bus wheel? Probably on some recall. 12. Something is awfully fishy inside the bus. Bonus 13. Everyone knows a smart cowboy never sits under a full vulture with its tail up.

Page 23.   1–E, 2–A, 3–D, 4–I, 5–G (with second and third toes removed by toe-hold traps), 6–H, 7–C, 8–F, 9–B (the seldom seen four-toed). Animals that cross a road are on their beaten track and often found dead in their tracks.

Page 24. Hey reader! Want a bonus match game? Match these states with their state marine mammals.

Alaska	Right Whale
California	Bottlenose Dolphin
Connecticut	Humpback Whale
Florida	Gray Whale
Georgia/Massachusetts	Sperm Whale
Hawaii	Manatee
Mississippi	Bowhead Whale

Answer: Alaska—bowhead whale; California—gray whale; Connecticut—sperm whale; Florida—manatee; Georgia/Massachusetts—right whale; Hawaii—humpback whale; Mississippi—bottlenose dolphin.

PS: If you use this information to win a bar bet, send ol' Buck half in a plain brown envelope, c/o of the publisher. Do not mark "cash enclosed" on the envelope.

Page 26. All are true, but number 2 applies only in suburban Connecticut.

Page 28. Average animal life expectancies are approximates. Generally speaking, larger animals live longer. Most females of a species live longer and, she might add, much happier after the old man is gone. 1–G, 2–M, 3–H, 4–L, 5–B, 6–F, 7–A, 8–D, 9–E, 10–J, 11–I, 12–K, 13–C. In suburbia, reduce years by 75 percent. In greater Atlanta area, reduce years by 90 percent.

Page 29. 1–E, 2–D, 3–A, 4–C, 5–B.

Page 30. The large dog is a Chesapeake Bay retriever belonging to illustrator "Sourdough" McLean.

Page 31. All are true but number 2.

Page 34. The bottom two are both sides of the tissue.

Page 39. The top scene shows wildlife before suburban sprawl. The bottom scene shows suburban sprawl and suburban wildlife. The horror! The horror!

Page 43. All are true but number 20.

Page 45. **Across:** 1. Red BADGE of Courage. 4. CATSUP. 6. Red CROSS. 8. Red INK. 9. Red EYE. 10. Red CAP. 12. Red OAK. 13. Red HANDED. **Down:** 2. Red ANT. 3. Hunt for Red OCTOBER. 5. Red PONY. 6. Red CARPET. 7. Red SKELETON. 11. Red ROSE.

PS: At no small risk, the back of a real bear was used for this puzzle.

Page 51. 1–B, 2–C, 3–D, 4–G, 5–I, 6–A, 7–E (Editor's note: I can't find "mooseling" in any dictionary. Suspect author trying to pull a fast one. Hold his check.), 8–F (live birth), 9–J, 10–H.

Page 53. All are true, but number 8 could be false. All in-laws are squirrely, especially at reunions and other gift-giving occasions.

Page 58. 1. rattlesnake, 2. cottonmouth snake, 3. bull snake, and 4. garter snake.

Page 59. Sorry. In many suburbs, Bambi won't make it home to Mom.

Page 61. All are true, but number 8. See number 2. And that little yap-yap finally gets what it deserves. Wait until Wolfgang gets a taste for cat.

Pages 62 and 63. What's wrong with these answer pages? Nothing. Just a little dis- and a little dat information.

THE END OF THE ROAD

How did you like this coloring and activity book? Write to us at Roadkill USA, c/o Ten Speed Press, PO Box 7123, Berkeley, CA 94707. Be sure to order Buck's companion culinary books, THE ORIGINAL ROADKILL COOKBOOK and THE TOTALED ROADKILL COOKBOOK, from www.tenspeed.com

Don't forget to visit Buck, Sourdough, and Dorothy, Buck's hunting pig, at www.buckpeterson.com